This record book belongs to _____

School _____   Phone _____

Grade _____   Room _____   Year _____

Contents

Record student names across the top.

Records dates of assessments or use a section for each quarter of the year.

Record individual proficiencies at each date. You may choose to use any system, such as check marks, a 1–4 rubric, letters, or grades.

	Cara Avery				Luis Diaz				Sam Edwards				Jay|	
	9/6	9/8	10/15	2/3	9/6	9/8	10/15	2/3	9/6	9/8	10/15	2/3	9/6	9/
1.OA.A.1	1	1	2	2	3	3	3	4	1	2	2	3	2	3
	- struggles with comparing unknowns - needs support with word problems				- successful with all types of problems				- needs help decoding word problems				- strugg subtra	

Add detailed notes throughout the year.

For a more comprehensive resource guide with tips and additional reproducibles, visit *activities.carsondellosa.com*.

ISBN 978-1-4838-1112-3
01-135147784

Represent and solve problems involving addition and subtraction.

1.OA.A.1 Use addition and subtraction within 20 to solve word problems involving situations of adding to, taking from, putting together, taking apart, and comparing, with unknowns in all positions.

1.OA.A.2 Solve word problems that call for addition of three whole numbers whose sum is less than or equal to 20.

Understand and apply properties of operations and the relationship between addition and subtraction.

1.OA.B.3 Apply properties of operations as strategies to add and subtract.

1.OA.B.4 Understand subtraction as an unknown-addend problem.

Add and subtract within 20.

1.OA.C.5 Relate counting to addition and subtraction.

1.OA.C.6 Add and subtract within 20, demonstrating fluency for addition and subtraction within 10. Use strategies such as counting on; making ten; decomposing a number leading to a ten; using the relationship between addition and subtraction; and creating equivalent but easier or known sums.

Work with addition and subtraction equations.

1.OA.D.7 Understand the meaning of the equal sign, and determine if equations involving addition and subtraction are true or false.

1.OA.D.8 Determine the unknown whole number in an addition or subtraction equation relating three whole numbers.

Extend the counting sequence.

1.NBT.A.1 Count to 120, starting at any number less than 120. In this range, read and write numerals and represent a number of objects with a written numeral.

Understand place value.

1.NBT.B.2 Understand that the two digits of a two-digit number represent amounts of tens and ones. Understand the following as special cases:

1.NBT.B.2a 10 can be thought of as a bundle of ten ones—called a "ten."

1.NBT.B.2b The numbers from 11 to 19 are composed of a ten and one, two, three, four, five, six, seven, eight, or nine ones.

1.NBT.B.2c The numbers 10, 20, 30, 40, 50, 60, 70, 80, 90 refer to one, two, three, four, five, six, seven, eight, or nine tens (and 0 ones).

1.NBT.B.3 Compare two two-digit numbers based on meanings of the tens and ones digits, recording the results of comparisons with the symbols >, =, and <.

Use place value understanding and properties of operations to add and subtract.

1.NBT.C.4 Add within 100, including adding a two-digit number and a one-digit number, and adding a two-digit number and a multiple of 10, using concrete models or drawings and strategies based on place value, properties of operations, and/or the relationship between addition and subtraction; relate the strategy to a written method and explain the reasoning used. Understand that in adding two-digit numbers, one adds tens and tens, ones and ones; and sometimes it is necessary to compose a ten.

1.NBT.C.5 Given a two-digit number, mentally find 10 more or 10 less than the number, without having to count; explain the reasoning used.

1.NBT.C.6 Subtract multiples of 10 in the range 10–90 from multiples of 10 in the range 10–90 (positive or zero differences), using concrete models or drawings and strategies based on place value, properties of operations, and/or the relationship between addition and subtraction; relate the strategy to a written method and explain the reasoning used.

Measure lengths indirectly and by iterating length units.

1.MD.A.1 Order three objects by length; compare the lengths of two objects indirectly by using a third object.

1.MD.A.2 Express the length of an object as a whole number of length units, by laying multiple copies of a shorter object (the length unit) end to end; understand that the length measurement of an object is the number of same-size length units that span it with no gaps or overlaps. Limit to contexts where the object being measured is spanned by a whole number of length units with no gaps or overlaps.

Tell and write time.

1.MD.B.3 Tell and write time in hours and half-hours using analog and digital clocks.

Represent and interpret data.

1.MD.C.4 Organize, represent, and interpret data with up to three categories; ask and answer questions about the total number of data points, how many in each category, and how many more or less are in one category than in another.

Reason with shapes and their attributes.

1.G.A.1 Distinguish between defining attributes versus non-defining attributes; build and draw shapes to possess defining attributes.

1.G.A.2 Compose two-dimensional shapes (rectangles, squares, trapezoids, triangles, half-circles, and quarter-circles) or three-dimensional shapes (cubes, right rectangular prisms, right circular cones, and right circular cylinders) to create a composite shape, and compose new shapes from the composite shape.

1.G.A.3 Partition circles and rectangles into two and four equal shares, describe the shares using the words *halves*, *fourths*, and *quarters*, and use the phrases *half of*, *fourth of*, and *quarter of*. Describe the whole as two of, or four of the shares. Understand for these examples that decomposing into more equal shares creates smaller shares.

Language Arts Standards At a Glance

Key Ideas and Details

RL.1.1 Ask and answer questions about key details in a text.

RL.1.2 Retell stories, including key details, and demonstrate understanding of their central message or lesson.

RL.1.3 Describe characters, settings, and major events in a story, using key details.

Craft and Structure

RL.1.4 Identify words and phrases in stories or poems that suggest feelings or appeal to the senses.

RL.1.5 Explain major differences between books that tell stories and books that give information, drawing on a wide reading of a range of text types.

RL.1.6 Identify who is telling the story at various points in a text.

Integration of Knowledge and Ideas

RL.1.7 Use illustrations and details in a story to describe its characters, setting, or events.

RL.1.8 (not applicable to literature)

RL.1.9 Compare and contrast the adventures and experiences of characters in stories.

Range of Reading and Level of Text Complexity

RL.1.10 With prompting and support, read prose and poetry of appropriate complexity for grade 1.

Key Ideas and Details

RI.1.1 Ask and answer questions about key details in a text.

RI.1.2 Identify the main topic and retell key details of a text.

RI.1.3 Describe the connection between two individuals, events, ideas, or pieces of information in a text.

Craft and Structure

RI.1.4 Ask and answer questions to help determine or clarify the meaning of words and phrases in a text.

RI.1.5 Know and use various text features to locate key facts or information in a text.

RI.1.6 Distinguish between information provided by pictures or other illustrations and information provided by the words in a text.

Integration of Knowledge and Ideas

RI.1.7 Use the illustrations and details in a text to describe its key ideas.

RI.1.8 Identify the reasons an author gives to support points in a text.

RI.1.9 Identify basic similarities in and differences between two texts on the same topic.

Range of Reading and Level of Text Complexity

RI.1.10 With prompting and support, read informational texts appropriately complex for grade 1.

Print Concepts

RF.1.1 Demonstrate understanding of the organization and basic features of print.

> **RF.1.1a** Recognize the distinguishing features of a sentence.

> **RF.K.1b** Recognize that spoken words are represented in written language by specific sequences of letters.

Phonological Awareness

RF.K.2 Demonstrate understanding of spoken words, syllables, and sounds (phonemes).

> **RF.1.2a** Distinguish long from short vowel sounds in spoken single-syllable words.

> **RF.1.2b** Orally produce single-syllable words by blending sounds (phonemes), including consonant blends.

> **RF.1.2c** Isolate and pronounce initial, medial vowel, and final sounds (phonemes) in spoken single-syllable words.

> **RF.1.2d** Segment spoken single-syllable words into their complete sequence of individual sounds (phonemes).

Phonics and Word Recognition

RF.1.3 Know and apply grade-level phonics and word analysis skills in decoding words.

> **RF.1.3a** Know the spelling-sound correspondences for common consonant digraphs.

> **RF.1.3b** Decode regularly spelled one-syllable words.

> **RF.1.3c** Know final -e and common vowel team conventions for representing long vowel sounds.

> **RF.1.3d** Use knowledge that every syllable must have a vowel sound to determine the number of syllables in a printed word.

> **RF.1.3e** Decode two-syllable words following basic patterns by breaking the words into syllables.

> **RF.1.3f** Read words with inflectional endings.

> **RF.1.3g** Recognize and read grade-appropriate irregularly spelled words.

Fluency

RF.1.4 Read with sufficient accuracy and fluency to support comprehension.

> **RF.1.4a** Read grade-level text with purpose and understanding.

> **RF.1.4b** Read grade-level text orally with accuracy, appropriate rate, and expression on successive readings.

> **RF.1.4c** Use context to confirm or self-correct word recognition and understanding, rereading as necessary.

Text Types and Purposes

W.1.1 Write opinion pieces in which they introduce the topic or name the book they are writing about, state an opinion, supply a reason for the opinion, and provide some sense of closure.

W.1.2 Write informative/explanatory texts in which they name a topic, supply some facts about the topic, and provide some sense of closure.

W.1.3 Write narratives in which they recount two or more appropriately sequenced events, include some details regarding what happened, use temporal words to signal event order, and provide some sense of closure.

Production and Distribution of Writing

W.1.4 (begins in grade 3)

W.1.5 With guidance and support from adults, focus on a topic, respond to questions and suggestions from peers, and add details to strengthen writing as needed.

W.1.6 With guidance and support from adults, use a variety of digital tools to produce and publish writing, including in collaboration with peers.

Research to Build and Present Knowledge

W.1.7 Participate in shared research and writing projects.

W.1.8 With guidance and support from adults, recall information from experiences or gather information from provided sources to answer a question.

W.1.9 (begins in grade 4)

Range of Writing

W.1.10 (begins in grade 3)

Comprehension and Collaboration

SL.1.1 Participate in collaborative conversations with diverse partners about *grade 1 topics and texts* with peers and adults in small and larger groups.

SL.1.1a Follow agreed-upon rules for discussions.

SL.1.1b Build on others' talk in conversations by responding to the comments of others through multiple exchanges.

SL.1.1c Ask questions to clear up any confusion about the topics and texts under discussion.

SL.1.2 Ask and answer questions about key details in a text read aloud or information presented orally or through other media.

SL.1.3 Ask and answer questions about what a speaker says in order to gather additional information or clarify something that is not understood.

Presentation of Knowledge and Ideas

SL.1.4 Describe people, places, things, and events with relevant details, expressing ideas and feelings clearly.

SL.1.5 Add drawings or other visual displays to descriptions when appropriate to clarify ideas, thoughts, and feelings.

SL.1.6 Produce complete sentences when appropriate to task and situation.

Conventions of Standard English

L.1.1 Demonstrate command of the conventions of standard English grammar and usage when writing or speaking.

L.1.1a Print all upper- and lowercase letters.

L.1.1b Use common, proper, and possessive nouns.

L.1.1c Use singular and plural nouns with matching verbs in basic sentences.

L.1.1d Use personal, possessive, and indefinite pronouns.

L.1.1e Use verbs to convey a sense of past, present, and future.

L.1.1f Use frequently occurring adjectives.

L.1.1g Use frequently occurring conjunctions.

L.1.1h Use determiners.

L.1.1i Use frequently occurring prepositions.

L.1.1j Produce and expand complete simple and compound declarative, interrogative, imperative, and exclamatory sentences in response to prompts.

L.1.2 Demonstrate command of the conventions of standard English capitalization, punctuation, and spelling when writing.

L.1.2a Capitalize dates and names of people.

L.1.2b Use end punctuation for sentences.

L.1.2c Use commas in dates and to separate single words in a series.

L.1.2d Use conventional spelling for words with common spelling patterns and for frequently occurring irregular words.

L.1.2e Spell untaught words phonetically, drawing on. phonemic awareness and spelling conventions

Knowledge of Language

L.1.3 (begins in grade 2)

Vocabulary Acquisition and Use

L.1.4 Determine or clarify the meaning of unknown and multiple-meaning words and phrases based on *grade 1 reading and content*, choosing flexibly from an array of strategies.

L.1.4a Use sentence-level context as a clue to the meaning of a word or phrase.

L.1.4b Use frequently occurring affixes as a clue to the meaning of a word.

L.1.4c Identify frequently occurring root words and their inflectional forms.

L.1.5 With guidance and support from adults, demonstrate understanding of word relationships and nuances in word meanings.

L.1.5a Sort words into categories to gain a sense of the concepts the categories represent.

L.1.5b Define words by category and by one or more key attributes.

L.1.5c Identify real-life connections between words and their use.

L.1.5d Distinguish shades of meaning among verbs differing in manner and adjectives differing in intensity by defining or choosing them or by acting out the meanings.

L.1.6 Use words and phrases acquired through conversations, reading and being read to, and responding to texts, including using frequently occurring conjunctions to signal simple relationships.

Operations and Algebraic Thinking

1.OA.A.1 Use addition and subtraction within 20 to solve word problems involving situations of adding to, taking from, putting together, taking apart, and comparing, with unknowns in all positions, e.g., by using objects, drawings, and equations with a symbol for the unknown number to represent the problem.

1.OA.A.2 Solve word problems that call for addition of three whole numbers whose sum is less than or equal to 20, e.g., by using objects, drawings, and equations with a symbol for the unknown number to represent the problem.

1.OA.B.3 Apply properties of operations as strategies to add and subtract. *Examples: If 8 + 3 = 11 is known, then 3 + 8 = 11 is also known. (Commutative property of addition.) To add 2 + 6 + 4, the second two numbers can be added to make a ten, so 2 + 6 + 4 = 2 + 10 = 12. (Associative property of addition.)*

1.OA.B.4 Understand subtraction as an unknown-addend problem. *For example, subtract 10 − 8 by finding the number that makes 10 when added to 8.*

1.OA.C.5 Relate counting to addition and subtraction (e.g., by counting on 2 to add 2).

1.OA.C.6 Add and subtract within 20, demonstrating fluency for addition and subtraction within 10. Use strategies such as counting on; making ten (e.g., 8 + 6 = 8 + 2 + 4 = 10 + 4 = 14); decomposing a number leading to a ten (e.g., 13 − 4 = 13 − 3 − 1 = 10 − 1 = 9); using the relationship between addition and subtraction (e.g., knowing that 8 + 4 = 12, one knows 12 − 8 = 4); and creating equivalent but easier or known sums (e.g., adding 6 + 7 by creating the known equivalent 6 + 6 + 1 = 12 + 1 = 13).

1.OA.D.7 Understand the meaning of the equal sign, and determine if equations involving addition and subtraction are true or false. *For example, which of the following equations are true and which are false? 6 = 6, 7 = 8 − 1, 5 + 2 = 2 + 5, 4 + 1 = 5 + 2.*

1.OA.D.8 Determine the unknown whole number in an addition or subtraction equation relating three whole numbers. *For example, determine the unknown number that makes the equation true in each of the equations 8 + ? = 11, 5 = ☐ − 3, 6 + 6 = ☐.*

_____

_____

_____

_____

Standards Crosswalk

Kindergarten
Operations and Algebraic Thinking
Understand addition as putting together and adding to, and understand subtraction as taking apart and taking from.
- Represent and express addition and subtraction with various methods.
- Use addition and subtraction within 10 to solve word problems.
- Decompose numbers 1–10 into pairs in more than one way.
- Find the number that makes 10 when added to a given number.
- Fluently add and subtract within 5.

Understand and apply properties of operations and the relationship between addition and subtraction.
- Apply properties of operations as strategies to add and subtract.
- Understand subtraction as an unknown-addend problem.

Add and subtract within 20.
- Relate counting to addition and subtraction.
- Use strategies to add and subtract within 20.
- Demonstrate fluency with addition and subtraction within 10.

Work with addition and subtraction equations.
- Understand the meaning of the equal sign.
- Determine if addition and subtraction equations are true or false.
- Find the unknown number in addition and subtraction equations.

Second Grade
Operations and Algebraic Thinking
Represent and solve problems involving addition and subtraction.
- Use addition and subtraction within 100 to solve one- and two-step word problems with unknowns in all positions (including those represented by a symbol).

Add and subtract within 20.
- Fluently add and subtract within 20 using mental strategies.
- Memorize all sums of two one-digit numbers.

Work with equal groups of objects to gain foundations for multiplication.
- Determine if a group of up to 20 objects represents an odd or even number.
- Use addition to find the total number of objects arranged in rectangular arrays with up to five rows and up to five columns.
- Write an equation to express the sum of an array.

1.OA.A.1

1.OA.A.2

1.OA.B.3

1.OA.B.4

1.OA.C.5

1.OA.C.6

1.OA.D.7

1.OA.D.8

1.OA.A.1																			
1.OA.A.2																			
1.OA.B.3																			
1.OA.B.4																			
1.OA.C.5																			
1.OA.C.6																			
1.OA.D.7																			
1.OA.D.8																			

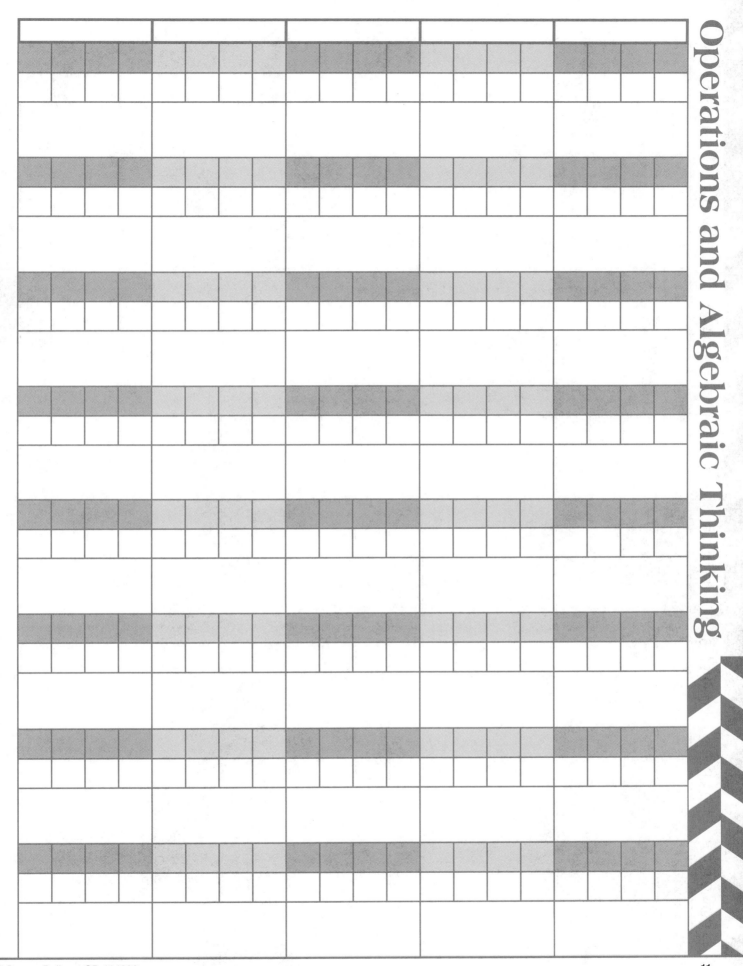

1.OA.A.1									
1.OA.A.2									
1.OA.B.3									
1.OA.B.4									
1.OA.C.5									
1.OA.C.6									
1.OA.D.7									
1.OA.D.8									

Number and Operations in Base Ten

1.NBT.A.1 Count to 120, starting at any number less than 120. In this range, read and write numerals and represent a number of objects with a written numeral.

1.NBT.B.2 Understand that the two digits of a two-digit number represent amounts of tens and ones. Understand the following as special cases:

1.NBT.B.2a 10 can be thought of as a bundle of ten ones—called a "ten."

1.NBT.B.2b The numbers from 11 to 19 are composed of a ten and one, two, three, four, five, six, seven, eight, or nine ones.

1.NBT.B.2c The numbers 10, 20, 30, 40, 50, 60, 70, 80, 90 refer to one, two, three, four, five, six, seven, eight, or nine tens (and 0 ones).

1.NBT.B.3 Compare two two-digit numbers based on meanings of the tens and ones digits, recording the results of comparisons with the symbols >, =, and <.

1.NBT.C.4 Add within 100, including adding a two-digit number and a one-digit number, and adding a two-digit number and a multiple of 10, using concrete models or drawings and strategies based on place value, properties of operations, and/or the relationship between addition and subtraction; relate the strategy to a written method and explain the reasoning used. Understand that in adding two-digit numbers, one adds tens and tens, ones and ones; and sometimes it is necessary to compose a ten.

1.NBT.C.5 Given a two-digit number, mentally find 10 more or 10 less than the number, without having to count; explain the reasoning used.

1.NBT.C.6 Subtract multiples of 10 in the range 10–90 from multiples of 10 in the range 10–90 (positive or zero differences), using concrete models or drawings and strategies based on place value, properties of operations, and/or the relationship between addition and subtraction; relate the strategy to a written method and explain the reasoning used.

Standards Crosswalk

Kindergarten

Counting and Cardinality

Know number names and the count sequence.
- Count to 100 by ones and tens.
- Count forward from a given number.
- Write and represent numbers from 0–20.

Count to tell the number of objects.
- Understand the relationship between numbers and quantities.
- Count to answer "how many?" questions up to 20 objects in a formation or up to 10 scattered objects.
- Count out a given number of objects from 1–20.

Compare numbers.
- Compare two groups of objects and identify them as greater than, less than, or equal to one another.
- Compare two written numerals between 1 and 10.

Number and Operations in Base Ten

Work with numbers 11–19 to gain foundations for place value.
- Compose and decompose numbers from 11 to 19 into tens and ones and record by drawings or equations.

Second Grade

Number and Operations in Base Ten

Understand place value.
- Understand that the digits of a three-digit number represent amounts of hundreds, tens, and ones.
- 100 can be thought of as a bundle of 10 tens, or a "hundred".
- The multiples of 100 (through 900) refer to 1–9 hundreds, 0 tens, and 0 ones.
- Count within 1000.
- Skip-count by 5s, 10s, and 100s.
- Read and write numbers to 1000 using numerals, number names, and expanded form.
- Use >, =, and < to compare two three-digit numbers.

Use place value understanding and properties of operations to add and subtract.
- Fluently add and subtract within 100.
- Add up to four two-digit numbers.
- Add and subtract within 1000, relating the strategies used to a written method.
- Mentally add or subtract 10 or 100 to or from a given number 100–900.
- Explain why addition and subtraction strategies work.

1.NBT.A.1																			
1.NBT.B.2																			
1.NBT.B.3																			
1.NBT.C.4																			
1.NBT.C.5																			
1.NBT.C.6																			

1.NBT.A.1

1.NBT.B.2

1.NBT.B.3

1.NBT.C.4

1.NBT.C.5

1.NBT.C.6

1.NBT.A.1																			
1.NBT.B.2																			
1.NBT.B.3																			
1.NBT.C.4																			
1.NBT.C.5																			
1.NBT.C.6																			

Notes

Notes

Measurement and Data

1.MD.A.1 Order three objects by length; compare the lengths of two objects indirectly by using a third object.

1.MD.A.2 Express the length of an object as a whole number of length units, by laying multiple copies of a shorter object (the length unit) end to end; understand that the length measurement of an object is the number of same-size length units that span it with no gaps or overlaps. *Limit to contexts where the object being measured is spanned by a whole number of length units with no gaps or overlaps.*

1.MD.B.3 Tell and write time in hours and half-hours using analog and digital clocks.

1.MD.C.4 Organize, represent, and interpret data with up to three categories; ask and answer questions about the total number of data points, how many in each category, and how many more or less are in one category than in another.

Kindergarten
Measurement and Data
Describe and compare measurable attributes.
- Understand what can be measured.
- Compare two objects using a measurable attribute to determine which has more of or less of the attribute.

Classify objects and count the number of objects in each category.
- Classify and sort objects into categories.
- Count the total in each category and sort by count.

Second Grade
Measurement and Data
Measure and estimate lengths in standard units.
- Measure the length of an object by selecting and using appropriate tools.
- Measure the length of an object using two different length units and relate the measurements to the units used.
- Estimate lengths using units of inches, feet, centimeters, and meters.
- Measure to determine how much longer one object is than another.

Relate addition and subtraction to length.
- Use addition and subtraction within 100 to solve word problems involving lengths given in the same units.
- Represent whole numbers as lengths from 0 on a number line and represent whole-number sums and differences within 100 on a number line.

Work with time and money.
- Tell and write time from analog and digital clocks to the nearest five minutes, using am and pm.
- Solve word problems involving dollar bills, quarters, dimes, nickels, and pennies, using $ and ¢ symbols appropriately.

Represent and interpret data.
- Measure objects and represent measurements on a line plot (to the nearest whole unit).
- Draw a picture graph and a bar graph (with single-unit scales) to represent up to four categories.
- Solve simple addition, subtraction, and comparison problems using information given in a graph.

1.MD.A.1

1.MD.A.2

1.MD.B.3

1.MD.C.4

1.MD.A.1

1.MD.A.2

1.MD.B.3

1.MD.C.4

1.MD.A.1

1.MD.A.2

1.MD.B.3

1.MD.C.4

Geometry

1.G.A.1 Distinguish between defining attributes (e.g., triangles are closed and three-sided) versus non-defining attributes (e.g., color, orientation, overall size); build and draw shapes to possess defining attributes.

1.G.A.2 Compose two-dimensional shapes (rectangles, squares, trapezoids, triangles, half-circles, and quarter-circles) or three-dimensional shapes (cubes, right rectangular prisms, right circular cones, and right circular cylinders) to create a composite shape, and compose new shapes from the composite shape.

1.G.A.3 Partition circles and rectangles into two and four equal shares, describe the shares using the words *halves*, *fourths*, and *quarters*, and use the phrases *half of*, *fourth of*, and *quarter of*. Describe the whole as two of, or four of the shares. Understand for these examples that decomposing into more equal shares creates smaller shares.

Standards Crosswalk

Kindergarten
Geometry

Identify and describe shapes (squares, circles, triangles, rectangles, hexagons, cubes, cones, cylinders, and spheres).
- Describe, name, and identify objects in the environment using shape names.
- Describe the relative position of objects.
- Correctly name shapes regardless of size or orientation.
- Identify plane (2-D) and solid shapes (3-D).

Analyze, compare, create, and compose shapes.
- Describe, analyze, and compare two- and three-dimensional shapes and their attributes.
- Model real-world shapes by building and drawing them.
- Combine simple shapes to form larger shapes.

Second Grade
Geometry

Reason with shapes and their attributes.
- Recognize and draw shapes with specific attributes.
- Identify triangles, quadrilaterals, pentagons, hexagons, and cubes.
- Partition a rectangle into rows and columns of same-size squares and count to find the total number of them.
- Partition circles and rectangles into two, three, or four equal shares, using the words *halves*, *thirds*, *half of*, *a fourth of*, etc., to describe them.
- Describe a divided whole as two halves, three thirds, four fourths.
- Recognize that equal shares of identical wholes may not have the same shape.

1.G.A.1																				
1.G.A.2																				
1.G.A.3																				

34

© Carson-Dellosa CD-104800

1.G.A.1

1.G.A.2

1.G.A.3

1.G.A.1

1.G.A.2

1.G.A.3

Notes

Notes

Reading Standards for Literature

RL.1.1 Ask and answer questions about key details in a text.

RL.1.2 Retell stories, including key details, and demonstrate understanding of their central message or lesson.

RL.1.3 Describe characters, settings, and major events in a story, using key details.

RL.1.4 Identify words and phrases in stories or poems that suggest feelings or appeal to the senses.

RL.1.5 Explain major differences between books that tell stories and books that give information, drawing on a wide reading of a range of text types.

RL.1.6 Identify who is telling the story at various points in a text.

RL.1.7 Use illustrations and details in a story to describe its characters, setting, or events.

RL.1.8 (not applicable to literature)

RL.1.9 Compare and contrast the adventures and experiences of characters in stories.

RL.1.10 With prompting and support, read prose and poetry of appropriate complexity for grade 1.

Standards Crosswalk

Kindergarten

Reading: Literature

Key Ideas and Details

With prompting and support:
- Ask and answer questions about key details in a text.
- Retell familiar stories, including key details.
- Identify characters, settings, and major events in a story.

Craft and Structure
- Ask and answer questions about unknown words in a text.
- Recognize common types of texts.
- With prompting and support, name the author and illustrator of a story and define their roles in telling the story.

Integration of Knowledge and Ideas

With prompting and support:
- Describe the relationship between illustrations and the story.
- Compare and contrast the experiences of characters in familiar stories.

Range of Reading and Level of Text Complexity
- Participate in group reading activities with purpose and understanding.

Second Grade

Reading: Literature

Key Ideas and Details
- Ask and answer such questions as who, what, where, when, why, and how about key details in a text.
- Recount stories, including fables and folktales from diverse cultures, and determine their central messages, lessons, or morals.
- Describe how characters in a story respond to major events and challenges.

Craft and Structure
- Describe how words and phrases supply rhythm and meaning in a story, poem, or song.
- Describe the overall structure of a story.
- Understand the purpose of a story's beginning and ending.
- Acknowledge differences in the points of view of characters.
- Use different voices for each character when reading dialogue aloud.

Integration of Knowledge and Ideas
- Use information from illustrations and words in text to demonstrate understanding of its characters, setting, or plot.
- Compare and contrast two or more versions of the same story by different authors or from different cultures.

Range of Reading and Level of Text Complexity
- By the end of the year, proficiently read and comprehend literature in the grades 2–3 text complexity band.

RL.1.1

RL.1.2

RL.1.3

RL.1.4

RL.1.5

RL.1.6

RL.1.7

RL.1.9

RL.1.10

RL.1.1																			
RL.1.2																			
RL.1.3																			
RL.1.4																			
RL.1.5																			
RL.1.6																			
RL.1.7																			
RL.1.9																			
RL.1.10																			

RL.1.1																			
RL.1.2																			
RL.1.3																			
RL.1.4																			
RL.1.5																			
RL.1.6																			
RL.1.7																			
RL.1.9																			
RL.1.10																			

48

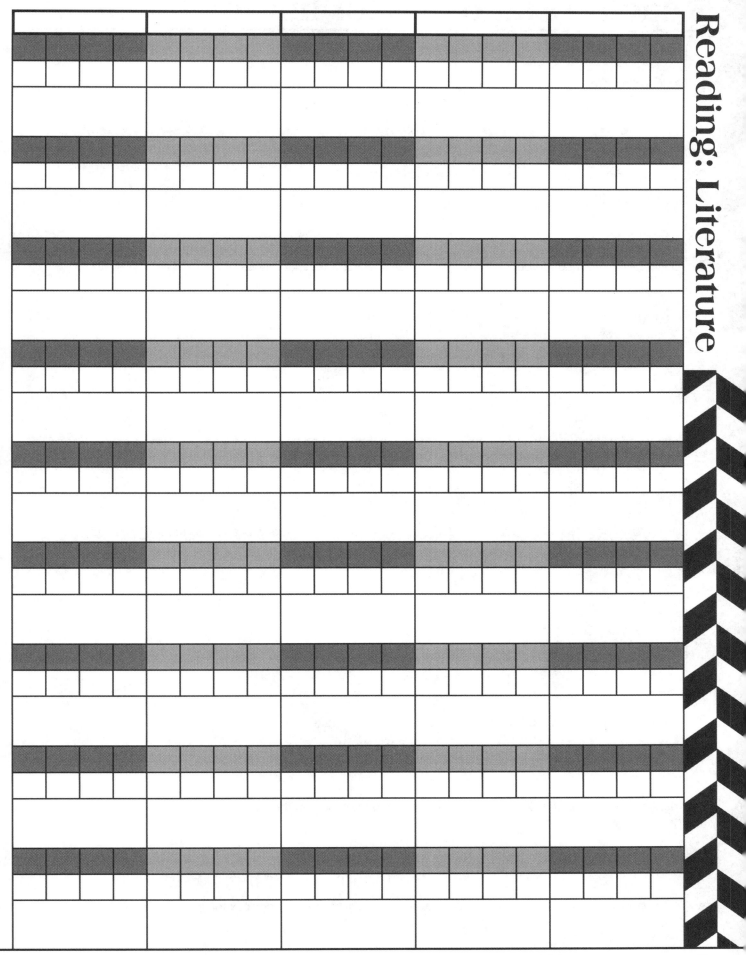

Reading Standards for Informational Text

RI.1.1 — Ask and answer questions about key details in a text.

RI.1.2 — Identify the main topic and retell key details of a text.

RI.1.3 — Describe the connection between two individuals, events, ideas, or pieces of information in a text.

RI.1.4 — Ask and answer questions to help determine or clarify the meaning of words and phrases in a text.

RI.1.5 — Know and use various text features (e.g., headings, tables of contents, glossaries, electronic menus, icons) to locate key facts or information in a text.

RI.1.6 — Distinguish between information provided by pictures or other illustrations and information provided by the words in a text.

RI.1.7 — Use the illustrations and details in a text to describe its key ideas.

RI.1.8 — Identify the reasons an author gives to support points in a text.

RI.1.9 — Identify basic similarities in and differences between two texts on the same topic (e.g., in illustrations, descriptions, or procedures).

RI.1.10 — With prompting and support, read informational texts appropriately complex for grade 1.

Standards Crosswalk

Kindergarten
Reading: Informational Text

Key Ideas and Details

With prompting and support:
- Ask and answer questions about key details in a text.
- Identify the main topic and retell key details of a text.
- Describe the connection between two individuals, events, ideas, or pieces of information in a text.

Craft and Structure
- Ask and answer questions about unknown words in a text.
- Identify the front cover, back cover, and title page of a book.
- Name the author and illustrator of a text and define their roles.

Integration of Knowledge and Ideas

With prompting and support:
- Describe the relationship between illustrations and the text.
- Identify the reasons an author gives to support points in a text.
- Identify basic similarities and differences between two texts on the same topic.

Range of Reading and Level of Text Complexity
- Participate in group reading activities with purpose and understanding.

Second Grade
Reading: Informational Text

Key Ideas and Details
- Ask and answer questions such as who, what, where, when, why, and how about key details in a text.
- Identify the main topic of a multi-paragraph text and the focus of specific paragraphs.
- Describe the connection between a series of historical events, scientific ideas or concepts, or steps in technical procedures in a text.

Craft and Structure
- Determine the meaning of words and phrases in a text.
- Use text features (captions, bold print, subheadings, glossaries, indexes, electronic menus, icons) to locate information.
- Identify the main purpose of a text, including the author's purpose.

Integration of Knowledge and Ideas
- Explain how specific images contribute to and clarify a text.
- Describe how reasons support specific points made in a text.
- Compare and contrast key points presented by two texts on the same topic.

Reading and Level of Text Complexity
- By the end of the year, read and comprehend informational texts in the grades 2-3 complexity band.

RI.1.1					
RI.1.2					
RI.1.3					
RI.1.4					
RI.1.5					
RI.1.6					
RI.1.7					
RI.1.8					
RI.1.9					
RI.1.10					

52

RI.1.1																			
RI.1.2																			
RI.1.3																			
RI.1.4																			
RI.1.5																			
RI.1.6																			
RI.1.7																			
RI.1.8																			
RI.1.9																			
RI.1.10																			

RI.1.1					
RI.1.2					
RI.1.3					
RI.1.4					
RI.1.5					
RI.1.6					
RI.1.7					
RI.1.8					
RI.1.9					
RI.1.10					

Reading Standards: Foundational Skills

RF.1.1

Demonstrate understanding of the organization and basic features of print.
- RF.1.1a Recognize the distinguishing features of a sentence (e.g., first word, capitalization, ending punctuation).
- RF.K.1b Recognize that spoken words are represented in written language by specific sequences of letters.

RF.1.2

Demonstrate understanding of spoken words, syllables, and sounds (phonemes).
- RF.1.2a Distinguish long from short vowel sounds in spoken single-syllable words.
- RF.1.2b Orally produce single-syllable words by blending sounds (phonemes), including consonant blends.
- RF.1.2c Isolate and pronounce initial, medial vowel, and final sounds (phonemes) in spoken single-syllable words.
- RF.1.2d Segment spoken single-syllable words into their complete sequence of individual sounds (phonemes).

RF.1.3

Know and apply grade-level phonics and word analysis skills in decoding words.
- RF.1.3a Know the spelling-sound correspondences for common consonant digraphs.
- RF.1.3b Decode regularly spelled one-syllable words.
- RF.1.3c Know final -e and common vowel team conventions for representing long vowel sounds.
- RF.1.3d Use knowledge that every syllable must have a vowel sound to determine the number of syllables in a printed word.
- RF.1.3e Decode two-syllable words following basic patterns by breaking the words into syllables.
- RF.1.3f Read words with inflectional endings.
- RF.1.3g Recognize and read grade-appropriate irregularly spelled words.

RF.1.4

Read with sufficient accuracy and fluency to support comprehension.
- RF.1.4a Read grade-level text with purpose and understanding.
- RF.1.4b Read grade-level text orally with accuracy, appropriate rate, and expression on successive readings.
- RF.1.4c Use context to confirm or self-correct word recognition and understanding, rereading as necessary.

Standards Crosswalk

Kindergarten

Reading: Foundational Skills

Print Concepts
- Follow words from left to right, top to bottom, and page by page.
- Recognize that spoken words are represented in written language by specific sequences of letters.
- Understand that words are separated by spaces in print.
- Recognize and name all upper- and lowercase letters of the alphabet.

Phonological Awareness
- Understand spoken words, syllables, and phonemes.
- Recognize and produce rhyming words.
- Count, pronounce, blend, and segment syllables in spoken words.
- Blend and segment onsets and rimes of single-syllable spoken words.
- Isolate and pronounce the initial, medial vowel, and final sounds in three-phoneme (CVC) words.
- Add or substitute individual sounds in one-syllable words to make new words.

Phonics and Word Recognition
- Know and apply grade-level phonics and word analysis skills in decoding words.
- Apply knowledge of one-to-one letter-sound correspondences by producing the primary sound or most frequent sounds for each consonant.
- Associate the long and short sounds with the common spellings for major vowels.
- Read common sight words.
- Distinguish between similarly spelled words by identifying the sounds that differ.

Fluency
- Read emergent-reader texts with purpose and understanding.

Second Grade

Reading: Foundational Skills

Print Concepts and Phonological Awareness ends in first grade.

Phonics and Word Recognition
- Know and apply grade-level phonics and word analysis skills.
- Identify long and short vowels in regularly spelled one-syllable words.
- Know spelling-sound correspondences for additional common vowel teams.
- Decode regularly spelled two-syllable words with long vowels.
- Decode words with common prefixes and suffixes.
- Identify words with inconsistent but common spelling-sound correspondences.
- Recognize and read grade-appropriate irregularly spelled words.

Fluency
- Read with sufficient accuracy and fluency to support comprehension.
- Read grade-level text with purpose and understanding.
- Read grade-level text orally with accuracy, appropriate rate, and expression on successive readings.
- Use context and rereading to confirm or self-correct word recognition and understanding.

RF.1.1

RF.1.2

RF.1.3

RF.1.4

RF.1.1				
RF.1.2				
RF.1.3				
RF.1.4				

RF.1.1																			
RF.1.2																			
RF.1.3																			
RF.1.4																			

Notes

Notes

Writing

W.1.1 Write opinion pieces in which they introduce the topic or name the book they are writing about, state an opinion, supply a reason for the opinion, and provide some sense of closure.

W.1.2 Write informative/explanatory texts in which they name a topic, supply some facts about the topic, and provide some sense of closure.

W.1.3 Write narratives in which they recount two or more appropriately sequenced events, include some details regarding what happened, use temporal words to signal event order, and provide some sense of closure.

W.1.4 (begins in grade 3)

W.1.5 With guidance and support from adults, focus on a topic, respond to questions and suggestions from peers, and add details to strengthen writing as needed.

W.1.6 With guidance and support from adults, use a variety of digital tools to produce and publish writing, including in collaboration with peers.

W.1.7 Participate in shared research and writing projects (e.g., explore a number of "how-to" books on a given topic and use them to write a sequence of instructions).

W.1.8 With guidance and support from adults, recall information from experiences or gather information from provided sources to answer a question.

W.1.9 (begins in grade 4)

W.1.10 (begins in grade 3)

Standards Crosswalk

Kindergarten
Writing

Text Types and Purposes
- Use a combination of drawing, dictating, and writing to compose opinion pieces that tell a reader the topic or the name of the book they are writing about; state an opinion or preference about the topic or book.
- Use a combination of drawing, dictating, and writing to compose informative/explanatory texts that name what they are writing about and supply information about the topic.
- Use a combination of drawing, dictating, and writing to narrate a single event or several loosely linked events in the correct order, and provide a reaction to what happened.

Production and Distribution of Writing

With guidance and support:
- Respond to feedback from peers and add details to strengthen writing as needed.
- Explore a variety of digital tools to produce and publish writing, including in collaboration with peers.

Research to Build and Present Knowledge
- Participate in shared research and writing projects.
- With guidance and support, recall information from experiences or gather information from provided sources to answer a question.

Second Grade
Writing

Text Types and Purposes
- Write opinion pieces that introduce a topic or book, state an opinion, supply reasons to support the opinion, use linking words, and provide a concluding statement or section.
- Write informative/explanatory texts that introduce a topic, use facts and definitions to develop points, and provide a concluding statement or section.
- Write narratives that recount a well-elaborated event or short sequence of events; include details to describe actions, thoughts, and feelings; use temporal words to signal event order; and provide a sense of closure.

Production and Distribution of Writing

With guidance and support:
- Focus on a topic and strengthen writing as needed by revising and editing.
- Use a variety of digital tools to produce and publish writing, including in collaboration with peers.

Research to Build and Present Knowledge
- Participate in shared research and writing projects.
- Recall information from experiences or gather information from provided sources to answer a question.

Range of Writing begins in grade 3.

W.1.1																				
W.1.2																				
W.1.3																				
W.1.5																				
W.1.6																				
W.1.7																				
W.1.8																				

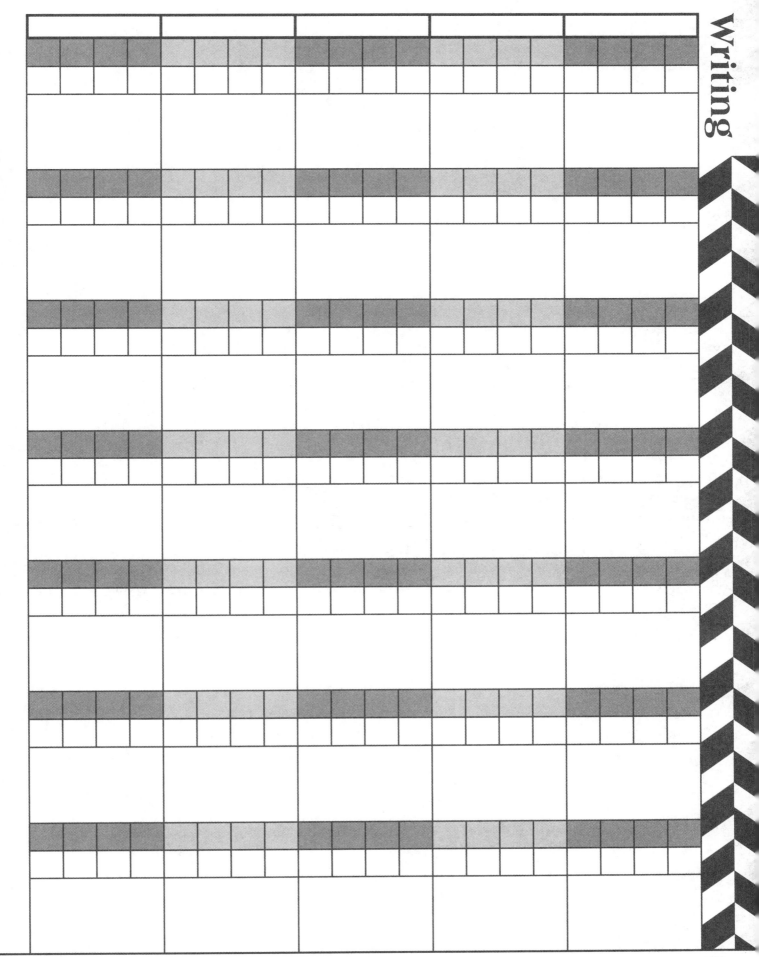

W.1.1																				
W.1.2																				
W.1.3																				
W.1.5																				
W.1.6																				
W.1.7																				
W.1.8																				

W.1.1					
W.1.2					
W.1.3					
W.1.5					
W.1.6					
W.1.7					
W.1.8					

74

Speaking and Listening Standards

SL.1.1 Participate in collaborative conversations with diverse partners about *grade 1 topics and texts* with peers and adults in small and larger groups.

    SL.1.1a Follow agreed-upon rules for discussions (e.g., listening to others with care, speaking one at a time about the topics and texts under discussion).

    SL.1.1b Build on others' talk in conversations by responding to the comments of others through multiple exchanges.

    SL.1.1c Ask questions to clear up any confusion about the topics and texts under discussion.

SL.1.2 Ask and answer questions about key details in a text read aloud or information presented orally or through other media.

SL.1.3 Ask and answer questions about what a speaker says in order to gather additional information or clarify something that is not understood.

SL.1.4 Describe people, places, things, and events with relevant details, expressing ideas and feelings clearly.

SL.1.5 Add drawings or other visual displays to descriptions when appropriate to clarify ideas, thoughts, and feelings.

SL.1.6 Produce complete sentences when appropriate to task and situation.

Standards Crosswalk

Kindergarten
Speaking and Listening

Comprehension and Collaboration
- Participate in group discussions about grade-appropriate topics and texts.
- Follow agreed upon discussion rules.
- Continue a conversation through multiple exchanges.
- Confirm understanding of a text or other information presented orally or through other media by asking and answering questions about key details and requesting clarification if needed.

Presentation of Knowledge and Ideas
- Describe familiar people, places, things, and events; with prompting and support, provide additional detail.
- Add drawings or visual displays to descriptions to provide additional detail.
- Speak audibly and express thoughts, feelings, and ideas clearly.

Second Grade
Speaking and Listening

Comprehension and Collaboration
- Participate in group discussions about grade-appropriate topics and texts.
- Follow agreed upon discussion rules.
- Comment on the remarks of others, and ask for clarification if needed.
- Recount or describe key ideas or details from a text or other channels of information.
- Ask and answer questions about a presentation to clarify comprehension, gather more information, or deepen understanding.

Presentation of Knowledge and Ideas
- Audibly and coherently tell a story or recount an experience with appropriate facts and relevant, descriptive details.
- Create audio recordings of stories or poems.
- Add drawings or other visual displays when appropriate.
- Produce complete sentences to provide requested detail or clarification.

SL.1.1																			
SL.1.2																			
SL.1.3																			
SL.1.4																			
SL.1.5																			
SL.1.6																			

SL.1.1				
SL.1.2				
SL.1.3				
SL.1.4				
SL.1.5				
SL.1.6				

SL.1.1																			
SL.1.2																			
SL.1.3																			
SL.1.4																			
SL.1.5																			
SL.1.6																			

82

Language

L.1.1

Demonstrate command of the conventions of standard English grammar and usage when writing or speaking.

L.1.1a Print all upper- and lowercase letters.

L.1.1b Use common, proper, and possessive nouns.

L.1.1c Use singular and plural nouns with matching verbs in basic sentences (e.g., *He hops*; *We hop*).

L.1.1d Use personal, possessive, and indefinite pronouns (e.g., *I, me, my*; *they, them, their, anyone, everything*).

L.1.1e Use verbs to convey a sense of past, present, and future (e.g., *Yesterday I walked home*; *Today I walk home*; *Tomorrow I will walk home*).

L.1.1f Use frequently occurring adjectives.

L.1.1g Use frequently occurring conjunctions (e.g., *and, but, or, so, because*).

L.1.1h Use determiners (e.g., articles, demonstratives).

L.1.1i Use frequently occurring prepositions (e.g., *during, beyond, toward*).

L.1.1j Produce and expand complete simple and compound declarative, interrogative, imperative, and exclamatory sentences in response to prompts.

L.1.2

Demonstrate command of the conventions of standard English capitalization, punctuation, and spelling when writing.

L.1.2a Capitalize dates and names of people.

L.1.2b Use end punctuation for sentences.

L.1.2c Use commas in dates and to separate single words in a series.

L.1.2d Use conventional spelling for words with common spelling patterns and for frequently occurring irregular words.

L.1.2e Spell untaught words phonetically, drawing on phonemic awareness and spelling conventions.

L.1.3

(begins in grade 2)

L.1.4

Determine or clarify the meaning of unknown and multiple-meaning words and phrases based on *grade 1 reading and content*, choosing flexibly from an array of strategies.

L.1.4a Use sentence-level context as a clue to the meaning of a word or phrase.

L.1.4b Use frequently occurring affixes as a clue to the meaning of a word.

L.1.4c Identify frequently occurring root words (e.g., *look*) and their inflectional forms (e.g., *looks, looked, looking*).

L.1.5

With guidance and support from adults, demonstrate understanding of word relationships and nuances in word meanings.

L.1.5a Sort words into categories (e.g., colors, clothing) to gain a sense of the concepts the categories represent.

L.1.5b Define words by category and by one or more key attributes (e.g., a *duck* is a bird that swims; a *tiger* is a large cat with stripes).

L.1.5c Identify real-life connections between words and their use (e.g., note places at home that are *cozy*).

L.1.5d Distinguish shades of meaning among verbs differing in manner (e.g., *look, peek, glance, stare, glare, scowl*) and adjectives differing in intensity (e.g., *large, gigantic*) by defining or choosing them or by acting out the meanings.

L.1.6

Use words and phrases acquired through conversations, reading and being read to, and responding to texts, including using frequently occurring conjunctions to signal simple relationships (e.g., *because*).

Standards Crosswalk

Kindergarten
Language
Conventions of Standard English
- Print many upper- and lowercase letters.
- Use frequently occurring nouns and verbs; form regular plural nouns orally by adding /s/ or /es/; understand and use question words; use the most frequently occurring prepositions.
- Produce and expand complete sentences in shared language activities.
- Capitalize the first word in a sentence; capitalize the pronoun I; recognize and name end punctuation.
- Write a letter or letters for most consonant and short-vowel sounds; spell simple words phonetically.

Knowledge of Language begins in grade 2.

Vocabulary Acquisition and Use
- Identify new meanings for familiar words.
- Use inflections and affixes as clues to word meaning.
- Sort common objects into categories.
- Relate frequently occurring verbs and adjectives to their opposites.
- Identify real-world connections between words and their use.
- Distinguish shades of meaning among similar verbs by acting them out.
- Use words and phrases acquired through conversations, reading and being read to, and responding to texts.

Second Grade
Language
Conventions of Standard English
- Use collective nouns; form and use frequently occurring irregular plural nouns; use reflexive pronouns; form and use the past tense of common irregular verbs; use adjectives and adverbs appropriately.
- Produce, expand, and rearrange complete simple and compound sentences.
- Capitalize holidays, product names, and geographic names; use commas in greetings and closings of letters; use apostrophes to form contractions and frequently occurring possessives.
- Generalize learned spelling patterns when writing words; consult reference materials as needed to check and correct spellings.

Knowledge of Language
- Compare formal and informal uses of English.

Vocabulary Acquisition and Use
- Use sentence-level context as a clue to the meaning of a word or phrase.
- Determine meaning when a known prefix is added to a known word; use a known root word to determine an unknown word with the same root; use knowledge of individual words to predict the meaning of compound words; use glossaries and dictionaries to determine the meaning of new words.
- Identify real-world connections between words and their uses.
- Distinguish shades of meaning among related verbs and related adjectives.
- Use words and phrases (including descriptive adjectives and adverbs) acquired through conversations, reading and being read to, and responding to texts.

L.1.1				
L.1.2				
L.1.4				
L.1.5				
L.1.6				

L.1.1

L.1.2

L.1.4

L.1.5

L.1.6

L.1.1																				
L.1.2																				
L.1.4																				
L.1.5																				
L.1.6																				

Standard _____

Notes

Notes

Notes